*The Pigeon
Has Landed*

The Pigeon Has Landed

*A rich collection of
"pick and mix" verse to
engage and delight you*

JENNY CARO

Copyright © 2021 Jenny Caro

The moral right of the author has been asserted.

Apart from any fair dealing for the purposes of research or private study, or criticism or review, as permitted under the Copyright, Designs and Patents Act 1988, this publication may only be reproduced, stored or transmitted, in any form or by any means, with the prior permission in writing of the publishers, or in the case of reprographic reproduction in accordance with the terms of licences issued by the Copyright Licensing Agency. Enquiries concerning reproduction outside those terms should be sent to the publishers.

This is a work of fiction. Names, characters, businesses, places, events and incidents are either the products of the author's imagination or used in a fictitious manner. Any resemblance to actual persons, living or dead, or actual events is purely coincidental.

Matador
9 Priory Business Park,
Wistow Road, Kibworth Beauchamp,
Leicestershire. LE8 0RX
Tel: 0116 279 2299
Email: books@troubador.co.uk
Web: www.troubador.co.uk/matador
Twitter: @matadorbooks

ISBN 978 1800464 568

British Library Cataloguing in Publication Data.
A catalogue record for this book is available from the British Library.

Printed and bound by CPI Group (UK) Ltd, Croydon, CR0 4YY
Typeset in 11pt Adobe Garamond Pro by Troubador Publishing Ltd, Leicester, UK

Matador is an imprint of Troubador Publishing Ltd

This little book is for my dear husband Maurice and for our family – Jane, Andrea, Hugo, Louis, Maisie, Pearl and Iris.

Contents

The Solution	1
Contentment	2
A Nautical Ghost	4
Autumn Musings	5
Homage to Sewage	7
The Phantom Poet of Old London Town	9
Winter Stew	11
Love Food	12
Modern Nursery Rhyme	14
The Battered Crow – a Tale of Woe	15
Togetherness	17
Precious	18
Kindness	20
An Unkindness of Ravens	21
Light Into Dark	22
Sudden Wealth	24
The Crow	25
Comfit	27
First of October – Remembrance	29
Superstition	30
Winter Dusk	31
Back to the Drawing Board	32
Alone	33
Fancy Feeding	34

A Poem a Day	35
Heaven Knows	36
Street Light	38
Poisonous Beauty	39
Dances with Doggerels	40

Introduction

This little volume of verse is brought to you by one of the most amazing of birds on this planet – the humble pigeon. For many centuries, pigeons have been the best of friends to mankind. In times of war and other emergencies, these remarkable birds have delivered vital and life-saving messages swiftly and unerringly to their destination. Long may they live and flourish!

And long may you enjoy dipping into these verses!

The Solution

Don't tell me that you can't escape
The bullying that comes through your phone.
It's really so easy peasy, you know.
You shouldn't need to be shown.

Don't tell me you're feeling stressed
When your mobile is on all the while.
It's child's play, my friend, to switch it off.
The tension will go. You can smile!

You seem to think you're a total slave
To demands from your chosen ringtone.
The billionaires who invented this toy
Hook you in and won't leave you alone.

But you've got to show them who's the boss,
That you have a clear, cool head.
You're not prepared to be brainwashed
And act like the living dead.

Stop thinking your mobile's glued to your hand,
As if it's essential to life.
It's not. Turn it off and choose freedom instead!
Oh, joy! No more stress and strife.

Contentment

It's lovely to be old enough to be out of the swing of the tide.
To stay close in to the sheltering bank. To watch the younger ones ride
On the heltering, skeltering stream of life the all-powerful Fates decree.
To wish every youngster a safe journey as they follow their destiny.

After three score years and another ten, with their mixture of tears and laughter,
Our strongest urge is to leave the surge of living to those who come after.
We've learned who we are. We know what we've done. We have achieved some of our goals.
And now we've become content to leave the unfulfilled gaps in our souls.

It's a peaceful place – Nature's waiting room – if you welcome it with good grace.
And spend your time in quiet pursuits and savour the ambling pace.
If you realise that memories change as you age and a rose-tinted picture remains,
This metamorphosis of what you remember makes pleasures outnumber the pains.

A Nautical Ghost

An old sailor's ghost from times past
Whose hauntings were nothing but farce.
He'd been failing for years
To frighten his peers,
Just abseiling down the main mast.

And when the crew jeered him and said,
"We know who you are, AB Fred
So whatever you do
To frighten this crew
Will just make us yawn instead."

Oh dear, what an insult! Poor Fred!
He felt so embarrassed, went red.
Then slid down the ship's side,
Made a hole ten feet wide
And drowned all his shipmates – quite dead.

Autumn Musings

My Muse and I love the Autumn-tide.

When the trees are stripping bare – throwing off their coats so they can watch the blizzards of leaves dance earthwards in the blustering autumn gales. Gutters disappear under piles of multi-coloured leaves. The wind builds drifts of them on the pavement's edge, where they curl and crisp for our feet to joyfully crunch and kick their way through. It is a jolly time of year for all except for our stalwart street sweepers.

It is a time for celebrations when, as a last hurrah before Winter, English folk gather to the Goose Fairs and the fairground roundabouts on their common lands. Eager to fill themselves up with the joy of childish fun and entertainment – enough to last until the annual promises of Spring and Easter are fulfilled.

It is a soothing time when Nature blooms with the softly mauve and massed ranks of abundant daisies. They bloom so densely and joyfully on even the poorest land and are named to celebrate the feast day of St Michael the Archangel. He who hurled Lucifer down from Heaven into the depths of the underworld – oh, what a fall that was.

And then our dear Moon, huge in her perigee, comes peering over the fence of the horizon to visit her neighbour Earth. She comes not to borrow a cup of sugar, but to set the nocturnal world of Autumn ablaze with her dazzling light before winter's dark descends.

Homage to Sewage

*(Can be sung to the tune of "Sing
a Song of Sixpence")*

Sing a song of sewage,
Handle, chain and flush.
But mind you watch your language,
Don't make the readers blush.
Sewage works are wonders
In managing our waste.
Without them we would be neck deep
In excrement encased.

Sewage works can alter
The whiff of all our waste.
If not, the gross effluvia
Will fill us with distaste.
When processing has finished,
The final smell will be
The perfumes of Arabia
Sweet peas and rosemary.

Without our modern sewage works
Where would our wastage go?
I just can't bear to think of where
Our human sludge would flow.
Could be down our high streets?
Or on our motorways?
Imagine the M25
With a mellow chocolate glaze.

The Phantom Poet of Old London Town

There's a funny kind of rumour going round in London town
Of paranormal happenings far and near.
It seems a phantom poet is a-haunting of the place,
Though people say we do not have to fear.

The ghostly versifier who's never been ID'd
Is a past-master of disguise for every day.
On Monday a City banker, on Tuesday it's a punk
And then a busker warbling down our way.

Some London people, in the way that people do,
Have claimed to see this mystery bard.
The spectre is, they say, a ghastly sight to see
With flaming eyes that stare – they're rivet hard.

But after every sighting of this strange London fiend,
A calling card is found upon the shelves
Of every high street bookseller that you or I can name.
It smacks of ghosts or goblins, could be elves.
A card of devilish good poetry on a topic of the day
Is placed for folk to take and keep beside their bed.
And strangely all of those who've taken them away
Declare it's the best verse they've ever read.

So keep your eyes a-purling in a bookshop where you stray
And look for calling cards upon their shelves.
Take just the one and take it home for you to try your hand
At writing lots of wondrous verse yourselves.

Winter Stew

When having a bit of a winter
With sleet and snow and ice,
I was hoping that *Woman's Hour*
Would suggest some hot meals that were nice.

Instead I'm afraid that today's eating fads,
Which increasingly change recipes,
Can only come up with a nightmarish stew
Made of kale, mangelwurzels and peas.

So it's kale, peas and boomps a daisy!
Let's do the vegetable waltz.
The digestive results of this horrible dish
Will not bring you romance or schmaltz.

In fact it will ruin your prospects
Of ever finding success,
If you do not open both windows and doors
After eating this horrible mess.

Love Food

Never mind music, Will!
We're talking *food* of love, here.
We are looking for something more substantial than a stave of strange black symbols.
And anyway, a musician or three is not always handy at critical times!
So where's the food?

As you well know – in your own time and for many centuries earlier, aphrodisiac foods were known and universally used to spice up seduction and sharpen love-making abilities.
(Much nicer than those little blue tablets!)

And what a collation of exotic foods could be spread before you to achieve your desire.
The menu for your feast will, mayhap, begin with oysters and asparagus.
And then, be followed by eels with honey and hot chillies to raise your temperature to fever pitch.
At the height of the fever, make a libation to Aphrodite with sweet Malmsey wine before engaging on your venture. This will ensure a good and satisfying outcome.

And afterwards, restore and soothe yourself with watermelon served with honey-roasted pistachios.

Then, and only then, we might have music, Will, if you insist.

Modern Nursery Rhyme

Hush little baby, don't say a word.
Mummy's on her mobile and mustn't be disturbed.
The forty-two times that you called out her name,
I'm sorry to say fell on deaf ears again.

I'm trying to think of what you can do.
Have you tried shouting 'til your face turns blue?
The likelihood is that she still won't reply,
However much you shout and desperately cry.

My only words of comfort – you're not on your own.
A million UK babies are competing with a phone!

*The Battered Crow
– a Tale of Woe*

There was a knock upon my door.
I opened it at once and saw
A battered crow upon the floor.
He looked at me and muttered, "Caw,
I cannot fly nor walk no more.
My legs hurt most, my wings are sore
And when I saw your garden door
With ancient signs from days of yore
I knocked upon it to implore
A plea for pity for this poor
Old crow whose legs are red and raw."

"Dear Crow, I'm really sorry for
Your hurt and pain and wounds galore.
But tell me, tell me, I implore,
Whatever caused these wounds? I'm sure
It must have been a great raptor
With needle teeth and massive claw.
No prize for guessing any more,
It must have been a dinosaur.
Do you remember what you saw
When it attacked you on the floor?
Was it something you had seen before?"

Crow answered me – his voice in awe,
"The beast was covered in bloody gore.
He seemed to think he waged a war
And I the nearest enemy he saw."
With this, Crow slumped down on the floor
And lay lifeless, ah! for ever more.
I wept for his demise, I bore
His little corpse outside the door
And buried it with grave dolour.
Then a fervent oath I swore,
Never again to answer my door.

Togetherness

They sit knee to knee each side of a small table in the cafe.

Their eyes do not meet. Their eyes are glazed over and only see the images in their own heads. They shut us out.

They do not listen for the sound of the other's voice. Their ears are tuned to cyber wavelengths.

Their right arms are lifted up to ear level and pressing the plastic plaything onto their heads and holding it there.

Oh, the joy of a new togetherness! The unison using of mobile phones – so close and yet so far apart.

Precious

I laid down to rest and the rocks were hard against my back – even through the thick layers of winter clothes I was wearing.

The weather was cold and misty, the air laden with moisture. The grey sea lay a little way away and whispered quietly as it breathed and moved in and out.

Your weight on me was heavy, sudden and unexpected. We both lay there and were passive.
We did not speak.
How long we stayed there I don't know.
When we got up, we just resumed our winter walk along the beach.

Pondering on it afterwards, I welcomed the non-consummation.
I welcomed the absence of explanation as to why you laid your body on mine for that brief time and in that virginal manner.
And yet this was as close as I ever came to making love with you, my earliest true love.

Freezing the frame at that point of un-loving meant that my flimsy fancy of what true love was would be preserved forever. It could never be tainted by bodily thrashings. Just as the lives of those who die young are preserved and never change. My fancy has remained with me through long years now – untarnished and precious.

Kindness

It's kindly to offer the strength of your shoulder
And lend a sad soul a caring ear.
Such kindness can tell those who suffer alone
That someone has heard their fear.

To share what you have with those who have less,
Not just with your own kith and kin,
Can comfort a stranger's despairing soul
And make them feel hopeful again.

To speak friendly words to all that you meet
Or silently send a warm smile,
Can brighten the day of a struggling soul
As they tackle life's endless mile.

So take your genes of kindness,
The ones you were given at birth,
And use them each day as much as you can
To sweeten this sad old Earth.

An Unkindness of Ravens

What an awful collective noun
For the ravens of London town.
The ones at the Tower
Stand guard every hour
And strike all the other birds down.

Though keen to get their own back,
When the other birds plan an attack,
They find they're too craven
To tackle a raven,
Oh dear! Alas and alack!

Light Into Dark

I know you are in a dark place where you did not want to be.
That you never even imagined such a place existed when life was good to you.
When you had exciting things to do – your mind and imagination fully engaged.
When you had a family to love and cherish you, and you them.
And when you had friends, some old and some who were so recently strangers, to give you new ideas, to love, support and admire you for what you are.

When one special friend became more to you – an object of desire, a person to be close to and to give and share dreams with. Oh, how great and sweet a need was in you then.

Little did you realise what a perilous position you were in. Blinded by the light of this idol you worshipped, you could not see the cliff edge. How near it was and how close to it your beloved was. Then all the lights went out.

Where did all the lights go? you cried. Where's the light switch?

Silence – the darkness was implacable.

Sudden Wealth

"I really don't believe it!
How on Earth did that happen?" I cry.
I'd never have guessed
That I'd be so blessed
If a lottery ticket I'd buy.

I had never bought one before
But on impulse bought myself four.
The next thing I know
It's my numbers they show
And a million I've won. Maybe more!

I have no idea at all
What to do with this sudden windfall.
Spend the lot in one go?
Go mad? Splash the dough?
Or bury it deep after nightfall?

The Crow

I can just see him out of the corner of my left eye. He is some way away from me as I sit on the memorial bench in the cemetery. He waits and considers whether I am a danger to him. I freeze and half close my eyes so that he thinks I am not looking at him.

Ever so slowly I take from my bag the little biscuit which had been laid in the saucer of my coffee cup. Slowly and quietly I remove its clear wrapping and empty the broken pieces of biscuit into my right hand. I take three of the pieces and gently throw them onto the path in front of me. He watches warily but does not move.

I take the rest of the pieces and also gently throw them down too. Then I sit like a statue.

Crow starts to hop towards the biscuit pieces and me. The nearer he comes the clearer I see his roughish, roguish feathers and his knowing eyes, ever watchful.

Slowly he comes really close, makes a sudden dash to pick up one piece of biscuit, and instantly takes a short flight and eats it with relish at a safe distance.

He comes again – five or six more times he comes to seize a piece of biscuit and retreat to eat it.

Ah, too soon – the spell is broken. He flies away into the treetops. What pleasure in such a simple thing – leaving the world and my grief for half an hour to watch a beautiful crow.

Comfit

Of all the sweetest memories of times when I was young,
I put the liquorice comfit on the topmost rung.

When it came to spending my two pence, comfits won "hands down".
No other treats called out to me in the sweet shops of my town.

The bright and *motley* colours! Heaven knows what dyes they used.
But in those days we just loved the tastes and merrily we chewed.

These treats were double value – first the sugar shells to crack
Before you reached the liquorice that made your tongue turn black.

And did we have a favourite? Of course, and guess which one.
Why, the red that gave us lipstick and many hours of fun.

And when the great Torpedoes came – why, heaven itself was mine.
I could suck and crunch them happily until the end of time!

First of October – Remembrance

Every year that passes is one step closer to you.
I come to sit beside your grave and ponder the times we knew.

When side by side and hand in hand we shared life's rains and sun.
Rarely apart and not until your earthly span was done.

The years we spent together filled my soul to the brim.
Their legacy gives me comfort and peace, and our past is never dim.

It will last me with no shortage until my time has come
To leave this Earth and sleep by your side to the end of time, dearest one.

Superstition

Give me my lucky rabbit's foot,
I feel a disaster approaching!
And where is my four-leaf clover
To deal with my sense of foreboding?
I spilled some salt this morning
And threw it over my shoulder.
So I hope that its luck will stick to me
And make me feel much bolder.

If only a lucky black cat
Would cross my path today
And a bird would christen my noddle,
All my troubles will fade away.

Winter Dusk

The peace and quiet of a winter dusk is what my soul yearns for most,
For solitude or with a silent companion whose yearning matches my own.
The day is nearly spent – its bustle and noise have gone.
The sun is preparing to leave the scene – he's been busy from first birdsong
And he's now ready and willing to let the pale moon cast her cooling shadows on Earth.
Such balm for my troubled soul.

Back to the Drawing Board

It's all gone wrong again! Oh Lord!
All those efforts and no reward!
Should I fall upon my sword?
Or pull the communications cord?

How many more times must I try
To reach for the stars and fly too high?
Only, like Icarus, to fall from the sky
And bruise my ego once more.

Come on now, you can't afford
To abandon your quest – be eternally bored.
So grab your boot straps, pull hard,
Back once more to the drawing board.

Alone

I am alone but yet am not – for I walk with my thoughts.

The bliss of solitude is mine but not its pain – for I walk with my dreams.

One of the poor – yet all the world is mine.

Life is so sweet. Imagination, divine.

Fancy Feeding

Did you know that the waitress or waiter
Who serves up your jacket "potater"
Can signal quite clear
That they fancy you, dear,
And would like to serve you later.

You won't know the signs they use.
They tend to be small and hidden.
But the pepper grinder
Is a sure reminder
To watch out! It's something forbidden.

Did you know that the wine you select
Your state of mind can detect?
If it's white and quite dry
My dear, by and by,
They think that they're going to connect.

But if a merlot is your choice,
Conveyed in a dark, sexy voice,
The signal you're sending
Is more than befriending.
In fact just beware, don't rejoice!

A Poem a Day

A poem a day keeps the blues away.
It's not just the words and their meaning,
But the rhythm and rhyme
Must sound just fine
And in tune with the reader's feeling.

Choose an ode à la mode!
Avant-garde – I'm impressed!
Does it have to be any rhyme pattern?
Oh no, never fear!
An ode, my dear,
Can be any old classical Latin!

I fancy a verse that contains a curse
With a spell or a warlock within it.
Black sabbath and worse
Will provide a dire curse
That will never release or limit it.

Heaven Knows

(In the time of pandemic)

Heaven knows it's been a blitz of a year.
All lives transformed amid panic and fear.
Monopoly numbers announced every day
Of those infected and those passed away.

And it's Heaven that knows the *true* numbers who've died.
They've broken all records. Created a tide
Of human souls from across this vast Earth
That's past human telling – outnumbering births.

And how can we combat this hideous disease
That has left us floundering, brought to our knees?
Maybe we are not as bright as we thought
When it comes to an animal virus onslaught.

It isn't the only disaster we've had.
It arose after others that were almost as bad.
An invasion of locusts, huge floods and long drought,
And great fires that resisted attempts to put out.

It feels like a punishment – is it divine rage?
With Nemesis running amok in our age?
The primeval within us thinks we are cursed.
If so, then the outlook just couldn't be worse.

Let's look for the reasons behind this foul scourge.
Name all of our sins and begin a great purge
Of the damage and evil that mankind has wrought,
And start to reverse all the ruin we've brought.

The whole of our planet must be restored.
No Earth-dwelling element can be ignored.
We must stop being vandals to air, soil and seas,
To fauna and flora and all of our trees.

These huge transgressions must be put right
And the whole of mankind must commit to this fight.
We must not delay but start work with all speed.
Heaven knows we'll need miracles if we're to succeed.

Street Light

I met a smile beaming down my street this morning.

A spring-heeled black Adonis – tall, slender and garbed in the full regalia of today's streetwise young men – his was the smile.

He brought a lighthouse of joy to me and to all who saw him pass by on this sunless day.

Poisonous Beauty

There she stands in her prime showing off all her proud loveliness.
Her hair a dazzle of golden chains outshining everyone and everything.
Brilliant and so bright – reducing the rest of the world around her to dull, concrete grey.

But beware! For this stunning beauty is not what she seems.
Under that dazzling exterior lies a macabre and deadly secret.
Her entire interior is drenched in poison from her crown to her rooted feet.
Flowers, leaves, twigs, branches and roots.

Ask the great Architect of the world why he created such a beauty as a laburnum – a false, misleading tree.

Dances with Doggerels

(Can be sung to the tune of "Here We Go Looby Loo")

Doggerels love to dance,
Doggerels love to sing,
Doggerels love to prance
Round and round in a ring.

They do it when you're not looking,
They do not want you to know,
How good their fancy footwork is
And singing both high and low.

And when you're peacefully sleeping,
Thinking they're snug in their beds,
Doggerels dance a fandango
With tea towels on their heads.

Doggerels keep rehearsing,
They hope to be famous one day,
Selected to take part in *Strictly*
And carry the trophies away.

But even if they're not successful
Doggerels still will be there
To cheer you up on the grey days
And keep you from feeling despair.

Doggerels love to dance,
Doggerels love to sing,
Doggerels love to prance
Round and round in a ring!

For exclusive discounts on Matador titles,
sign up to our occasional newsletter at
troubador.co.uk/bookshop